dim sum

dim sum

VICKI LILEY

PERIPLUS
EDITIONS

contents

dim sum

foreword

A sure sign that a cuisine has evolved to its highest form is when its devotees refer to it as an art. Among the various Chinese cuisines, one way of eating has become a stylized and beautiful form of culinary art, though it is enjoyed within the din of a noisy restaurant. This is dim sum, or yum cha, and it has become part of the way we eat and socialize.

Not so long ago, the thought of meeting friends for breakfast or brunch was considered rather avant-garde. Now, across the world in cities where Cantonese people have settled, there is the marvelous tradition of meeting for dim sum. Dim sum charmingly translates as "to touch the heart," while yum cha means "to drink tea." Both having your heart touched and drinking tea are essential to this tradition, which began in the Guangzhou (Canton) region of China when teahouses started offering a few small snacks to attract locals and travelers. What was once an early form of "fast food" has evolved to a high level, with top dim sum chefs wooed to restaurants around the world, from Hong Kong to Sydney, Montreal to San Francisco.

Yum cha at its best is exquisite — the pretty little dim sum offerings almost too beautiful to eat, with some restaurants offering a couple hundred varieties. That beauty is governed by strict rules that are the same across the many styles of Chinese cuisine. The food must look exquisite, creating a visual harmony; it must smell delicious and tantalizing; it must taste as good as it looks and smells. These three things are equally important. The offering of a steaming basket or plate covered with a lid builds the suspense to the wonderful moment of seeing and smelling at the same time.

In Asia, especially Hong Kong, yum cha is offered from early morning to late afternoon. In other countries it's strictly a morning and lunchtime ritual. But what is changing is the "dim sum axis." Hong Kong's star is waning slightly with the economic downturn, and many top chefs are settling in Australia. It's fitting then that a dim sum cookbook has been created and photographed in Australia. For the book, expert chefs were asked to reveal their techniques and favorite recipes, from popular gow gees and dumplings to more unusual and more Western-influenced dishes such as salmon money bags and shrimp toast.

Some recipes, like lotus leaf wraps, are perfect to make ahead and impress your guests, combining, as they do, the Chinese trinity of visual harmony, aroma, and flavor. The lotus leaves are filled with short-grain rice mixed with slivers of mushrooms, Chinese sausage and king prawns (jumbo shrimp) and then steamed. They certainly achieve a "wow factor" when you cut through the leaf-wrapped bundles at the table, unleashing mouth-watering smells and revealing golden rice filled with delicious treats. After trekking across town every time the dim sum urge hits, it's reassuring to know that many favorites are easy to make at home. The recipes in this book were arranged by the talented and well-traveled Vicki Liley, and the photographs by Louise Lister are so good you want to eat them.

It's intriguing to note that this style of eating is continually evolving. From a chef's viewpoint dim sum is exciting. Among the many rules and recipes, there is still room to develop new dumplings and flaky little pies and little steamed baskets of goodies.

As more Westerners enjoy yum cha, new dishes sneak into the repertoire. Twenty years ago, dim sum always ended with custard tarts. Now there is a range of desserts such as fresh mango jelly and almond pudding.

There are rules to eating yum cha, which you'll notice if you sit anywhere near a Chinese table. The meal starts with the steamed dishes. Just as a chef balances flavors, thought should go into eating the series of small delicious dishes. Enjoy the tastes and combination of textures, the aromas of steaming tea and dumplings, the noise of yum cha trolleys clattering through the restaurant and the large parties enjoying their food and conversation. All this adds up to a most wonderful assault on the senses. What a terrific way to eat!

Maeve O'Meara is a Sydney-based food author and broadcaster who specializes in the many ethnic cuisines found in Australia.

dim sum

A Cantonese specialty, dim sum (variously translated as "dot hearts," "heart warmers" and "heart's delight") is the collective name for a variety of small, delicious snacks. It includes steamed or fried dumplings with meat or seafood fillings, steamed buns, shrimp balls and always a few desserts.

It is the Chinese custom to enjoy these tiny morsels with a pot or two of Chinese tea. Dim sum, or yum cha, as it is sometimes known, has become a tradition on Sunday mornings in most cities with a sizeable Chinese population. The little delicacies are displayed on trays and trolleys which pass by your table, tempting you to try them. Some trolleys are stacked with steaming buns in bamboo steamers, others with hot fried spring rolls and other "wrapped" dishes. The trolleys are brought around constantly so you need take only one or two dishes at a time and enjoy them when they're freshly cooked.

At home, dim sum is a different story: you can't possibly make the huge selection available to you in a restaurant. Instead choose two or three different dishes — most recipes can be prepared ahead of time, leaving the steaming or frying to be done at the last minute. All you need in the way of equipment is a wok and a bamboo steamer or two. Dim sum dishes can't be left sitting around: hot dishes should be served as hot as possible, and many are accompanied by soy sauce, chili sauce or one of the special dipping sauces on pages 100–105.

One or two dim sum dishes make an elegant and surprising appetizer to serve with drinks before dinner, and it is exceptional cocktail food (for a cocktail party of any size, you'll need a helper in the kitchen to keep the food coming). If you are serving a dim sum brunch, allow 8–10 bite-sized pieces per person and serve the food on small plates or in the steamers in which they are cooked. Set each place with a small bowl and chopsticks. Serve with Chinese tea.

tea

Chinese legend has it that, in 2737 B.C., the Emperor Chen-Nung discovered tea by accident one day while sipping boiled water in his garden. A few leaves fell from a tea bush into his cup, the emperor tasted it and liked it, and the tea drinking custom began.

By the fourth century A.D., tea was firmly established in China and was thought to have medicinal and restorative powers. The eighth-century poet Lu Yu wrote in the Cha King, or *Holy Scripture of Tea*, the first book ever written about tea, "... tea tempers the spirits, calms and harmonises the mind; it arouses thought and prevents drowsiness, lightens and refreshes the body, and clears the perceptive faculties."

Chinese tea is always served and consumed with dim sum. Milk or sugar is never added. When making Chinese tea, always select good-quality tea leaves and use only freshly boiled water. Traditionally, the Chinese use porcelain teapots and tiny porcelain cups without handles. Good teas can be infused three times — the second time is generally regarded as the best because, by then, the tea will release its full fragrance and aroma. About 1 teaspoon of tea is used to make one cup.

China tea may be classified into five varieties: scented, black, green, white and oolong.

Scented tea

Made from green tea, which is fully dried, then lightly scented with fragrant flowers. Scented tea is named after the flower with which it is scented — jasmine, orange bud, rose bud or white chrysanthemum.

Black tea

Fully fermented tea. The leaves turn black during the fermentation process.

Green tea

Manufactured without going through the process of fermentation. The natural emerald green color of the leaves is preserved.

White tea

A rare unfermented tea. The name "white" comes from the silvery-white color of the leaves.

Oolong tea

A semi-fermented tea combining the aromas and flavors of both green and black teas.

A wok is the perfect size and shape for steaming and deep-frying dim sum recipes. Carbon steel or rolled steel woks, the popular inexpensive vessels you see in Asian stores, are coated with a thin film of lacquer to prevent rusting. The film needs to be removed before the wok can be used. The best way to do this is to place the wok on the stove top, fill with cold water and add 2 tablespoons baking soda (bicarbonate of soda). Bring to the boil and boil rapidly for 15 minutes. Drain and scrub off the coating with a nylon pad. Repeat the process if any coating remains. Then rinse and dry the wok. It is now ready to be seasoned.

Carbon steel, rolled steel and cast-iron woks require seasoning before use, which creates a smooth surface that keeps food from sticking to it and prevents it from discoloring. To season a wok, place over low heat. Have paper towels and vegetable oil handy. When the wok is hot, carefully wipe it with an oiled paper towel. Repeat the process with fresh towels until they come away clean, without any trace of color.

A seasoned wok should not be scrubbed clean with detergent after cooking. Instead, use hot water and a sponge or nylon pad. Dry the wok well after washing, heat it gently, rub it over with an oiled paper towel and store in a dry, well-ventilated place. Long periods without use can cause the oil coating on the wok to become rancid. Using your wok is the best way to prevent this occurring.

There are a number of cooking utensils that go hand in hand with a wok. Bamboo steamers are available in many sizes at Asian supermarkets. They can be stacked on top of each other over a wok of simmering water, allowing the cook to prepare an entire meal at once or to cook the same dish in several batches. Bamboo steamers need only be rinsed in hot water after cooking. Allow them to dry thoroughly before storing. Other handy utensils are a slotted spoon or wire mesh skimmer for removing deep-fried foods from hot oil; a good-quality cleaver for chopping; and extra-long cooking chopsticks for stirring and lifting food.

Chinese dried mushrooms

Intensely flavorful, dark mushrooms that need to be rehydrated before use. Soak, off heat, in boiling water for 10–15 minutes and squeeze dry before slicing or chopping; discard tough stems.

Bok choy

Bok choy

Asian variety of cabbage with thick, white stalks and mild-flavored, dark green leaves. Sizes of bunches vary, from longer than celery stalks to baby bok choy about 6 inches (15 cm) long. Also known as Chinese cabbage. If unavailable, use Chinese broccoli or choy sum.

Chinese broccoli

Bitter-tasting broccoli with white flowers. Also known as gai laan. Chinese broccoli and choy sum can be used in place of each other.

Chinese dried mushrooms

Chinese sausages

Choy sum

Popular and widely available Chinese green vegetable with yellow flowers and thin stalks. Every part of the mild-flavored vegetable can be used. Also known as flowering cabbage.

Chinese sausages (lop chong)

Smoked pork sausages that are highly seasoned and slightly sweet. They are dry in texture and usually red in color, and are sold in the refrigerated section of Asian butchers and supermarkets. They should be steamed for 15 minutes or baked before eating.

Choy sum

Hoisin sauce

Rice wine

Hoisin sauce

Sweet, thick Chinese sauce made from soybeans and also containing vinegar, sugar, chili peppers and other seasonings. It can be stored indefinitely in the refrigerator. Also called Chinese barbecue sauce.

Rice paper wrappers

Made from rice flour, water and salt, these brittle, paper-thin wrappers are dipped in water before being used to wrap fresh or cooked food. They are eaten raw or they can also be fried, providing a crisp and light casing.

Rice wine

Sweet, low-alcohol Chinese wine, also known as shaoxing wine or shaoxing yellow rice wine, made from fermented glutinous rice. Sake or dry sherry can be substituted.

Shiitake mushrooms

Meaty mushrooms with light or dark brown caps. Dried shiitakes, also available, need to be rehydrated. Soak, off heat, in boiling water for 10–15 minutes and squeeze dry before slicing or chopping.

Rice paper

Shiitake mushrooms

Sesame oil

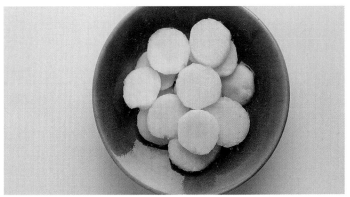

Water chestnuts

Sesame oil/Asian sesame oil

Strong-tasting oil pressed from roasted sesame seeds, mainly used as a flavoring. There is no substitute.

Spring roll wrappers

Thin sheets of rice flour dough, used to enclose savory fillings. They are rolled into a cigar shape and deep-fried until golden and crisp. Sometimes called spring roll skins, they are sold frozen in the supermarket. They should be defrosted and separated before using and covered with a damp kitchen towel while preparing.

Water chestnuts

Tuber of plant grown in Asia, round in shape with subtly sweet, crunchy, light-colored flesh. Water chestnuts are widely available canned; after opening, store in clean water in the refrigerator for up to 3 weeks. Also known as horses' hooves. If unavailable, use diced celery for a texture substitute.

Wonton wrapper

Thin sheets of wheat-based or egg-based dough, square or circular in shape, used to enclose a variety of fillings. Available fresh or frozen. Also called wonton skins, dumpling wrappers or gow gees. Fresh wrappers will keep for up to 7 days in the refrigerator. Wrappers may be frozen.

Spring roll wrappers

Wonton wrapper

methods

Step-by-step deep-frying

2. Working in batches, add food and fry until golden.

1. Pour required amount of oil into a large wok. Heat oil until it reaches 375°F (190°C) on a deep-frying thermometer or until a small bread cube dropped in oil sizzles and turns golden.

3. Use a wire mesh skimmer or slotted spoon to remove the food from the oil and drain on paper towels.

Step-by-step steaming

1. Line a medium bamboo steamer with parchment (baking paper), or cut individual pieces of parchment for dumplings and buns. Arrange food in steamer and cover with lid.

2. Half fill a medium wok with water (steamer should not touch water) and bring to the boil.

3. Place the steamer in the wok and steam for the required time, adding more boiling water to the wok when necessary. Lift the steamer off the wok and carefully remove the food.

NOTE: Bamboo steamers may be stacked on top of one another to cook several different dishes at the same time, or to cook the same dish in batches.

Step-by-step basic dumplings

1. Place round wonton wrappers onto a work surface and cover with a damp kitchen towel. Place wrapper on a work surface, spoon in filling, brush edges with water and fold in half to form a semicircle.

2. If you have a gow gee press, working with one wrapper at a time, lay it flat in the press and spoon filling into the center. Brush edges of wrapper with water. Close gow gee press firmly to seal edges together.

3. Square or round wonton wrappers can also be formed into little pouches around the filling. Pinch edges together to seal. Or gather edges around the filling to form a basket. Gently squeeze the center of the dumpling to expose the filling at the top. Tap the base of the dumpling on the work surface to flatten it. Set aside, covered with plastic wrap, while you make the remaining dumplings.

Step-by-step basic buns

1. Divide dough into walnut-sized rounds.

2. Roll or press each piece out to a circle. Cover dough with a damp kitchen towel.

3. Working with one dough round at a time, spoon filling into the center. Gather edges together and twist to seal dough. Cut out squares of parchment (baking paper) and place buns, sealed side down, onto paper.

classics

Golden shrimp balls

12 slices stale white bread

16 oz (500 g) jumbo shrimp (green king prawns),
   peeled and deveined

6 canned water chestnuts, drained and
   finely chopped

2 oz (60 g) bacon, rind removed and
   finely chopped

1 teaspoon sugar

1/2 teaspoon salt

2 teaspoons cornstarch (cornflour)

3 cups (24 fl oz/750 ml) vegetable oil for
   deep-frying

Remove crusts from bread. Cut bread into ¼-inch (6-mm) cubes. Spread out on a tray and allow to dry at room temperature.

Flatten shrimp with the back of a cleaver, then finely chop. Combine shrimp, water chestnuts and bacon in a bowl and stir in sugar, salt and cornstarch. Mix well. Cover and chill for 30 minutes.

Roll 1 tablespoon of shrimp mixture in bread cubes to coat. Repeat with remaining mixture. Heat oil in a large wok or saucepan until it reaches 375°F (190°C) on a deep-frying thermometer, or until a small bread cube dropped in oil sizzles and turns golden. Working in batches, add shrimp balls and fry until golden, 1–2 minutes. Using a slotted spoon, remove from oil and drain on paper towels. Serve hot with Quick Sweet-and-Sour Sauce (page 104).

Makes 12

GOLDEN SHRIMP BALLS

Flower dumplings

1 lb (500 g) ground (minced) chicken

6 canned water chestnuts, drained and
    finely chopped

1 small carrot, finely chopped

2 scallions (shallots/spring onions),
    finely chopped

1 teaspoon peeled and grated fresh ginger

1 teaspoon Asian sesame oil

1 teaspoon rice wine

1 teaspoon soy sauce

1 teaspoon salt

2 teaspoons sugar

2 tablespoons cornstarch (cornflour)

24 wonton wrappers

In a bowl, combine ground chicken, water chestnuts, carrot, scallions, ginger, sesame oil, rice wine, soy sauce, salt, sugar and cornstarch. Using wet hands, mix until well combined.

Place wonton wrappers on work surface and cover with a damp kitchen towel. Working with one wrapper at a time, lay it on work surface and place 3 teaspoons of chicken filling in the center. Gather edges around filling, forming a basket, and gently squeeze center of dumpling to expose the filling at the top. Tap bottom of dumpling on work surface to flatten. Cover with plastic wrap and set aside. Repeat with remaining wonton wrappers.

Line a medium bamboo steamer with parchment (baking paper). Half fill a medium wok with water (steamer should not touch water) and bring to a boil. Arrange filled wontons in steamer, cover, and place steamer over boiling water. Steam for 12 minutes, adding more boiling water to wok when necessary. Lift steamer off wok and carefully remove dumplings. Serve warm with soy sauce or Ginger Soy Dipping Sauce (page 100).

Makes 24

FLOWER DUMPLINGS

Pearl balls

1 cup (7 oz/220 g) short-grain white rice

1 lb (500 g) ground (minced) pork

4 scallions (shallots/spring onions), chopped

4 canned water chestnuts, drained and chopped

1 teaspoon sugar

1 teaspoon salt

2 cloves garlic, crushed

2 teaspoons grated fresh ginger

1 teaspoon Asian sesame oil

2 teaspoons light soy sauce

2 teaspoons rice wine

Place rice in a medium bowl. Cover with cold water and let stand for 30 minutes. Drain, spread out onto a paper towel–lined tray and allow to dry.

In a bowl, combine pork, scallions, water chestnuts, sugar, salt, garlic, ginger, sesame oil, soy sauce and rice wine. Using wet hands, mix until well combined. Divide mixture into 20 portions.

Line a bamboo steamer with banana leaves or parchment (baking paper). Using wet hands, shape pork mixture into small balls. Roll each ball in rice until well coated.

Half fill a medium wok with water (steamer should not touch water) and bring to a boil. Working in batches, arrange balls in prepared steamer, allowing room for rice to expand. Cover and place steamer over boiling water. Steam for 30 minutes, adding more boiling water to wok when necessary. Lift steamer off wok and carefully remove balls. Serve warm with soy sauce or Ginger Soy Dipping Sauce (page 100).

Makes about 20

PEARL BALLS

Stuffed crab claws

12 cooked crab claws

1 lb (500 g) jumbo shrimp (green king prawns), peeled and deveined

2 cloves garlic

3 teaspoons peeled and grated fresh ginger

1 egg white

2 teaspoons fish sauce

1/4 teaspoon salt

4 scallions (shallots/spring onions), roughly chopped

1/4 cup (1 1/2 oz/45 g) finely chopped celery

1/4 cup (1 oz/30 g) cornstarch (cornflour)

3 cups (24 fl oz/750 ml) vegetable oil for deep-frying

BATTER

1/2 cup (2 oz/60 g) cornstarch (cornflour)

1/2 cup (2 oz/60 g) all-purpose (plain) flour

1/2 teaspoon baking powder

1/2 teaspoon salt

1 cup (8 fl oz/250 ml) water

The shell around larger end of the crab claw is generally lightly cracked when purchased. Gently remove the shell, leaving shell on nipper end to make a handle for holding the crab claws.

Place shrimp, garlic, ginger, egg white, fish sauce and salt in a food processor and process until smooth. Transfer to a bowl. Stir in scallions and celery. Divide shrimp mixture into 12 portions. With wet hands, flatten each portion in palm of hand. Place flesh end of crab claw into center of shrimp mixture. Wrap shrimp around crab flesh. Wet hands again and mold shrimp evenly all over crab flesh.

To make batter, sift cornstarch, flour, baking powder and salt into a mixing bowl. Gradually add water, mixing to a smooth batter (this can also be done in a food processor).

Heat oil in a large wok or saucepan until it reaches 375°F (190°C) on a deep-frying thermometer, or until a small bread cube dropped in oil sizzles and turns golden. Dip crab claws in cornstarch, shaking off any excess. Working in batches and holding nipper end of crab claw, dip into batter. Fry until golden, 2–3 minutes. Using a slotted spoon, remove from oil and drain on paper towels. Serve hot with Chili Sauce (page 100) or Lime and Fish Sauce (page 105).

Makes 12

STUFFED CRAB CLAWS

Shrimp toasts

4 slices stale white bread

1 lb (500g) jumbo shrimp (green king prawns),
  peeled and deveined

2 cloves garlic

2 teaspoons peeled and grated fresh ginger

1 teaspoon sugar

1/2 teaspoon salt

1 tablespoon cornstarch (cornflour)

1 egg white

1 teaspoon Asian sesame oil

4 scallions (shallots/spring onions),
  finely chopped

1 egg, beaten

1 cup (4 oz/125 g) dry breadcrumbs

3 cups (24 fl oz/750ml) vegetable oil for
  deep-frying

*This Western-adapted recipe is a favorite in
most dim sum tea houses.*

Remove crusts from bread and cut each slice into 4 triangles. Allow bread to dry out at room temperature.

Place shrimp, garlic, ginger, sugar, salt, cornstarch, egg white and sesame oil in a food processor and process until smooth. Transfer to a bowl, then stir in scallions.

Place a tablespoon of shrimp filling in the center of each bread triangle. Brush shrimp filling and bread edges with beaten egg and sprinkle with breadcrumbs. Pat shrimp mixture into a pyramid shape, shaking off any excess crumbs.

Heat oil in a large wok until it reaches 375°F (190°C) on a deep-frying thermometer, or until a small bread cube dropped in oil sizzles and turns golden. Working in batches, fry toasts until golden on both sides, 1–2 minutes. Using a slotted spoon, remove from oil and drain on paper towels. Serve hot with Sweet Cilantro Sauce (page 102) or Quick Sweet-and-Sour Sauce (page 104).

Makes 14

SHRIMP TOASTS

Shanghai dumplings

1 lb (500 g) bok choy

1 lb (500 g) ground (minced) pork

1 tablespoon peeled and grated fresh ginger

1/4 teaspoon salt

1 teaspoon Asian sesame oil

1 teaspoon white vinegar

1 tablespoon oyster sauce

16 wonton wrappers

4 tablespoons vegetable oil

2/3 cup (5 fl oz/150 ml) water

Sometimes known as Shanghai street dumplings and originally made in the 1950s on the streets of Hong Kong on coal stoves by Shanghai refugees, these dumplings are still a favorite.

Cook bok choy in a pan of boiling water for 2 minutes, then drain and refresh in cold water. Finely chop bok choy. In a bowl, combine bok choy, pork, ginger, salt, sesame oil, vinegar and oyster sauce. Using wet hands, mix until well combined.

Place wonton wrappers on work surface and cover with a damp kitchen towel. Working with one wrapper at a time, lay it on work surface and place 3 teaspoons of pork filling in the center. Brush edges with water. Gather edges together and twist to seal. Place on a plate, sealed side down, cover with plastic wrap and set aside. Repeat with remaining wonton wrappers.

Heat 2 tablespoons oil in a wok or frying pan over medium heat. Working in batches, cook 8 dumplings, sealed side down, until golden, about 3 minutes. Carefully add half of water (liquid will sizzle and spatter a little; be careful) and cook until water evaporates. Reduce heat to low and continue to cook until dumplings are translucent, 3–4 minutes. Remove from pan. Repeat with remaining dumplings and remaining oil and water. Serve warm with soy sauce or Easy Plum Sauce (page 104).

Makes 16

SHANGHAI DUMPLINGS

Traditional mini spring rolls

2 tablespoons vegetable oil

2 cloves garlic, finely chopped

2 teaspoons peeled and grated fresh ginger

3 1/2 oz (100 g) ground (minced) pork

3 1/2 oz (100 g) ground (minced) chicken

2 oz (60 g) ground (minced) shrimp (prawns)

2 stalks celery, finely chopped

1 small carrot, finely chopped

6 canned water chestnuts, drained and finely chopped

4 scallions (shallots/spring onions), finely chopped

1 cup (3 oz/90 g) shredded Chinese cabbage

2 teaspoons cornstarch (cornflour)

2 tablespoon oyster sauce

1 tablespoon soy sauce

2 tablespoons chicken stock

1 teaspoon Asian sesame oil

20 frozen mini spring roll wrappers, about 4 1/2 inches
   (11.5 cm) square, thawed

2 teaspoons cornstarch (cornflour) mixed with
   2 tablespoons water

4 cups (32 fl oz/1 L) vegetable oil for deep-frying

Heat 1 tablespoon oil in a wok over medium heat. Add garlic and ginger, and cook until aromatic, about 1 minute. Stir in ground pork, chicken and shrimp, and cook, stirring, until mixture changes color, about 3 minutes. Remove from heat and transfer to a bowl.

Using same wok, heat remaining 1 tablespoon oil over medium heat. Add celery, carrot, water chestnuts, scallions and cabbage. Raise heat to high and stir-fry until softened, about 2 minutes. In a small bowl, combine cornstarch, oyster sauce, soy sauce and stock. Add to wok, bring to a boil, reduce heat to medium and cook until sauce thickens, 1–2 minutes. Remove from heat and allow to cool completely. Stir in cooled pork mixture and sesame oil, and mix well.

Separate spring roll wrappers, place on a work surface and cover with a damp kitchen towel. Working with one wrapper at a time, place on work surface and, using your fingertips, wet edges with cornstarch and water mixture. Place 1 tablespoon of filling in center of wrapper and roll up diagonally, tucking in edges. Seal edges with cornstarch mixture. Repeat with remaining wrappers.

Heat oil in a large wok until it reaches 375°F (190°C) on a deep-frying thermometer, or until a small bread cube dropped in oil sizzles and turns golden. Working in batches, add rolls and fry until golden, about 1 minute. Using a slotted spoon, remove from oil and drain on paper towels. Serve with Quick Sweet-and-Sour Sauce (page 104).

Makes 20

TRADITIONAL MINI SPRING ROLLS

Chinese pork sausage buns

1 cup (4 oz/125 g) self-rising flour

2 teaspoons baking powder

2 teaspoons superfine (caster) sugar

2 teaspoons lard

1/4–1/3 cup (2–3 fl oz/60–90 ml) warm milk

6 Chinese pork sausages

1 tablespoon hoisin sauce, plus extra for dipping

2 teaspoons soy sauce

Sift flour and baking powder into a bowl and add sugar. Rub lard into dry ingredients using your fingertips. Gradually add enough milk to make a soft dough. Turn dough out onto a floured work surface and knead for 1–2 minutes, until smooth. Wrap in plastic wrap and let stand for 30 minutes. Meanwhile, cut sausages in half crosswise. Place in a bowl with 1 tablespoon hoisin sauce and soy sauce, mix until well coated, cover, and let stand for 25 minutes.

Turn dough out onto a floured work surface and knead for 1 minute. Roll into a thick snake shape 12 inches (30 cm) long, and cut it into 12 pieces. Cover dough with a damp kitchen towel to prevent drying out. Working with one piece of dough at a time, rub it between floured hands to form a thin snake about 4 inches (10 cm) long. Wrap dough around sausage in a spiral pattern, leaving ends of sausage exposed, and place on an oiled tray. Repeat with remaining dough and sausages.

Line a bamboo steamer with banana leaves or parchment (baking paper). Half fill a medium wok with water (steamer should not touch water) and bring to a boil. Working in batches, arrange buns in prepared steamer, allowing room for buns to spread. Cover and place steamer over boiling water. Steam for 15 minutes, adding more boiling water to wok when necessary. Lift steamer off wok and carefully remove buns. Serve warm with hoisin sauce.

Makes 12

dumplings

Cook-and-sell dumplings

6 Chinese dried mushrooms

4 oz (125 g) jumbo shrimp (green king prawns),
  peeled, deveined and finely chopped

8 oz (250 g) ground (minced) pork

4 scallions (shallots/spring onions),
  finely chopped

1/2 teaspoon salt

1 teaspoon sugar

1 tablespoon oyster sauce

1 teaspoon Asian sesame oil

1 tablespoon cornstarch (cornflour)

12 wonton wrappers

These dumplings were traditionally cooked and sold on the streets, hence their name.

Place mushrooms in a small bowl, add boiling water to cover and let stand until softened, 10–15 minutes. Drain and squeeze excess liquid from mushrooms. Finely chop, discarding thick stems. In a bowl, combine mushrooms, shrimp, ground pork, scallions, salt, sugar, oyster sauce, sesame oil and cornstarch. Using wet hands, mix until well combined.

Place wonton wrappers on work surface and cover with a damp kitchen towel. Working with one wrapper at a time, lay it on work surface and place 2 teaspoons of filling in the center. Gather edges around filling, forming a basket, and gently squeeze center of dumpling to expose the filling at the top. Tap bottom of dumpling on work surface to flatten, cover with plastic wrap and set aside. Repeat with remaining wonton wrappers.

Line a medium bamboo steamer with parchment (baking paper). Half fill a medium wok with water (steamer should not touch water) and bring to a boil. Arrange filled wontons in steamer, cover and place steamer over boiling water. Steam for 10 minutes, adding more boiling water to wok when necessary. Lift steamer off wok and carefully remove dumplings. Serve warm with soy sauce or Ginger Soy Dipping Sauce (page 100).

Makes 12

Salmon money bags

9 oz (280 g) Atlantic salmon, bones and skin
   removed, finely chopped
3 tablespoons cream cheese
3 scallions (shallots/spring onions),
   finely chopped
2 teaspoons peeled and grated fresh ginger
¼ teaspoon salt
pinch five-spice powder
1 teaspoon grated lime zest
1 egg yolk
12 wonton wrappers
12 chives

This recipe is a tasty Western adaptation of the traditional favorite.

In a bowl, combine salmon, cream cheese, scallions, ginger, salt, five-spice powder, lime zest and egg yolk. Using wet hands, mix until well combined.

Place wonton wrappers on work surface and cover with a damp kitchen towel. Working with one wrapper at a time, lay it on work surface and place 2 teaspoons of filling in the center. Brush edges of wrapper with water. Gather edges together and twist to seal. Cover with a damp kitchen towel and set aside. Repeat with remaining wonton wrappers.

Line a medium bamboo steamer with parchment (baking paper). Half fill a medium wok with water (steamer should not touch water) and bring to a boil. Arrange filled wontons in steamer, cover and place steamer over boiling water. Steam for 8 minutes, adding more boiling water to wok when necessary. Lift steamer off wok and carefully remove dumplings. Dip chives into bowl of hot water and tie one loosely around the top of each money bag. Serve warm with soy sauce or Thai sweet chili sauce.

Makes 12

SALMON MONEY BAGS

Cockscomb dumplings

8 oz (250 g) ground (minced) chicken

4 scallions (shallots/spring onions), finely chopped

1 teaspoon peeled and grated fresh ginger

3 canned water chestnuts, drained and finely chopped

2 tablespoons finely chopped, drained canned bamboo shoots

2 teaspoons rice wine

2 teaspoons salt

1 teaspoon sugar

1 teaspoon soy sauce

1 teaspoon Asian sesame oil

1 tablespoon oyster sauce

1½ tablespoons cornstarch (cornflour)

16 round wonton wrappers

6 cups (48 fl oz/1.5 L) water

1 tablespoon vegetable oil

These dumplings are so named because they resemble the crest of a rooster.

In a bowl, combine ground chicken, scallions, ginger, water chestnuts, bamboo shoots, rice wine, 1 teaspoon salt, sugar, soy sauce, sesame oil, oyster sauce and cornstarch. Using wet hands, mix until well combined.

Place wonton wrappers on work surface and cover with a damp kitchen towel. Working with one wrapper at a time, place in a gow gee press and put 2 teaspoons of filling in the center. Brush edges of wrapper with water. Close gow gee press firmly to seal edges together. Alternatively, place wrapper on work surface, spoon in filling, brush with water and fold in half to form a semicircle. Pinch edges together to make a frill. Cover with a damp kitchen towel and repeat with remaining wrappers.

Pour water into a medium wok or saucepan, add remaining 1 teaspoon salt and vegetable oil, and bring to a boil. Working in batches, cook dumplings in boiling water for 5 minutes. Remove from pan with a slotted spoon. Run cold water over cooked dumplings. Serve immediately with Lime and Cilantro Dipping Sauce (page 103).

Makes 16

COCKSCOMB DUMPLINGS

Crisp-fried gow gee

6 Chinese dried mushrooms

4 oz (125 g) jumbo shrimp (green king prawns),
   peeled, deveined and finely chopped

8 oz (250 g) ground (minced) pork

½ cup (4 oz/125 g) finely chopped, drained
   canned bamboo shoots

6 scallions (shallots/spring onions),
   finely chopped

1 clove garlic, finely chopped

2 teaspoons Asian sesame oil

3 teaspoons soy sauce

2 teaspoons rice wine

20 round wonton wrappers

4 cups (32 fl oz/1 L) vegetable oil for deep-frying

Place mushrooms in a small bowl, add boiling water to cover and let stand until softened, 10–15 minutes. Drain and squeeze excess liquid from mushrooms. Finely chop, discarding thick stems. In a bowl, combine mushrooms, shrimp, ground pork, bamboo shoots, scallions, garlic, sesame oil, soy sauce and rice wine. Using wet hands, mix until well combined.

Place wonton wrappers on work surface and cover with a damp kitchen towel. Working with one wrapper at a time, place in a gow gee press and put 2 teaspoons of filling in the center. Brush edges of wrapper with water. Close gow gee press firmly to seal edges together. Alternatively, place wrapper on work surface, spoon in filling, brush with water and fold in half to form a semicircle. Pinch edges together to make a frill. Cover with a damp kitchen towel and repeat with remaining wrappers.

Heat oil in a large wok until it reaches 375°F (190°C) on a deep-frying thermometer, or until a small bread cube dropped in oil sizzles and turns golden. Working in batches, add gow gee and fry until golden on both sides, 1–2 minutes. Using a slotted spoon, remove from oil and drain on paper towels. Serve hot with soy sauce or Chili Sauce (page 100).

Makes 20

CRISP-FRIED GOW GEE

Pork swallows

8 oz (250 g) ground (minced) pork

4 oz (125 g) jumbo shrimp (green king prawns), peeled, deveined and finely chopped

1 tablespoon peeled and grated fresh ginger

4 scallions (shallots/spring onions), finely chopped

2 teaspoons rice wine

1/2 teaspoon salt

1 teaspoon Asian sesame oil

3 teaspoons cornstarch (cornflour)

20 square wonton wrappers

4 cups (32 fl oz/1 L) vegetable oil for deep-frying

Once fried, these tasty morsels resemble flying swallows.

Place ground pork, shrimp and ginger in a food processor and process until smooth. Transfer to a bowl. Add scallions, rice wine, salt, sesame oil and cornstarch. Using wet hands, mix until well combined.

Place wonton wrappers on work surface and cover with a damp kitchen towel. Working with one wrapper at a time, place 2 teaspoons of filling in the center and brush edges of wrapper with water. Fold wonton corners into the center, forming an envelope shape. Using your fingertips, press along diagonal edges to seal. Cover with a damp kitchen towel and repeat with remaining wrappers.

Heat oil in a large wok until it reaches 375°F (190°C) on a deep-frying thermometer, or until a small bread cube dropped in oil sizzles and turns golden. Working in batches, add wontons and fry until golden on both sides, 2–3 minutes. Using a slotted spoon, remove from oil and drain on paper towels. Serve hot with soy sauce or Lime and Cilantro Dipping Sauce (page 103).

Makes 20

Wok-fried money bags

1 bunch bok choy, washed and leaves separated

8 oz (250 g) ground (minced) chicken

1 teaspoon Asian sesame oil

3 scallions (shallots/spring onions), finely chopped

1 teaspoon peeled and grated fresh ginger

1 clove garlic, finely chopped

1 teaspoon rice wine

2 teaspoons oyster sauce

1 teaspoon soy sauce

pinch salt

3 teaspoons cornstarch (cornflour)

20 wonton wrappers

Money bags are shaped into little pouches gatered at the top, reminiscent of the little leather sacs used to carry money in China.

Cook bok choy in a pan of boiling water for 2 minutes. Drain, refresh in cold water and chop finely. In a bowl, combine bok choy, ground chicken, sesame oil, scallions, ginger, garlic, rice wine, oyster sauce, soy sauce, salt and cornstarch. Using wet hands, mix until well combined.

Place wonton wrappers on work surface and cover with a damp kitchen towel. Working with one wrapper at a time, place 2 teaspoons of filling in the center and brush edges of wrapper with water. Gather edges together and twist to seal. Cover with a damp kitchen towel and set aside. Repeat with remaining wonton wrappers.

Heat oil in a large wok until it reaches 375°F (190°C) on a deep-frying thermometer, or until a small bread cube dropped in oil sizzles and turns golden. Working in batches, add wontons and fry until golden, 1–2 minutes. Using a slotted spoon, remove from oil and drain on paper towels. Serve hot with soy, hoisin or plum sauce.

Makes 20

WOK-FRIED MONEY BAGS

Steamed spinach and ginger dumplings

1 tablespoon vegetable oil

1 tablespoon peeled and grated fresh ginger

3 cloves garlic, crushed

2 bunches spinach, washed and finely chopped

1/2 teaspoon salt

15 wonton wrappers

Heat oil in a wok or frying pan over medium heat. Add ginger and garlic, and stir-fry until aromatic, about 1 minute. Add spinach and stir-fry until soft, 2–3 minutes. Remove from heat and add salt. Transfer mixture to bowl and allow to cool completely.

Place wonton wrappers on work surface and cover with a damp kitchen towel. Working with one wrapper at a time, place 2 teaspoons of filling in the center and brush edges of wrapper with water. Gather edges together and twist to seal. Cover with a damp kitchen towel and set aside. Repeat with remaining wrappers.

Line a medium bamboo steamer with parchment (baking paper). Half fill a medium wok with water (steamer should not touch water) and bring to a boil. Arrange dumplings in steamer, cover and place steamer over boiling water. Steam for 10 minutes, adding more boiling water to wok when necessary. Lift steamer off wok and carefully remove dumplings. Serve warm with soy sauce.

Makes 15

STEAMED SPINACH AND GINGER DUMPLINGS

Snowpea shoot dumplings

4 oz (125 g) fresh snowpea (mange-tout) shoots, roughly chopped

4 oz (125 g) jumbo shrimp (green king prawns), peeled, deveined and coarsely chopped

2 teaspoons peeled and grated fresh ginger

3 teaspoons oyster sauce

1 teaspoon soy sauce

1 teaspoon rice wine

1/4 teaspoon salt

1/2 teaspoon sugar

1 teaspoon Asian sesame oil

1 tablespoon cornstarch (cornflour)

15 round wonton wrappers

Blanch snowpea shoots in a pan of boiling water for 1 minute. Drain and refresh immediately in cold water. In a bowl, combine snowpea shoots, shrimp, ginger, oyster sauce, soy sauce, rice wine, salt, sugar, sesame oil and cornstarch. Using wet hands, mix until well combined.

Place wonton wrappers on work surface and cover with a damp kitchen towel. Working with one wrapper at a time, place 3 teaspoons of filling in the center and brush edges of wrapper with water. Fold three sides of wrapper into the center, forming a triangular shape. Using your fingertips, press edges of wrapper together. Cover with a damp kitchen towel and set aside. Repeat with remaining wonton wrappers.

Line a medium bamboo steamer with parchment (baking paper). Half fill a medium wok with water (steamer should not touch water) and bring to a boil. Arrange dumplings in steamer, cover and place steamer over boiling water. Steam for 10 minutes, adding more boiling water to wok when necessary. Lift steamer off wok and carefully remove dumplings. Serve warm with soy sauce.

Makes 15

SNOWPEA SHOOT DUMPLINGS

Steamed pork buns

DOUGH

1½ teaspoons active dry yeast

½ cup (4 fl oz/125 ml) warm water

¼ cup (1¾ oz/50 g) superfine (caster) sugar

1 cup (4 oz/125 g) all-purpose (plain) flour

½ cup (2 oz/60 g) self-rising flour

3 teaspoons butter, melted

FILLING

2 tablespoons vegetable oil

3 teaspoons peeled and grated fresh ginger

2 cloves garlic, chopped

1 tablespoon hoisin sauce

1 tablespoon oyster sauce

1 tablespoon soy sauce

1 teaspoon Asian sesame oil

3 teaspoons cornstarch (cornflour) mixed with
   1 tablespoon water

8 oz (250 g) Chinese barbecue pork,
   finely chopped

6 scallions (shallots/spring onions),
   finely chopped

To make dough, in a small bowl combine yeast with 2 tablespoons warm water, 1 teaspoon sugar and 1 teaspoon all-purpose flour. Mix until well combined. Cover with a kitchen towel and let stand in a warm place until frothy, about 15 minutes.

Sift remaining all-purpose and self-rising flour into a large bowl. Add remaining sugar, yeast mixture, remaining warm water and melted butter. Using a wooden spoon, mix to form a soft dough. Turn out onto a floured work surface and knead until smooth and elastic, 3–5 minutes. Place dough in a large oiled bowl, cover and let stand in a warm place until doubled in bulk, about 1 hour.

To make filling, heat oil in a wok or frying pan over medium heat and fry ginger and garlic until aromatic, about 1 minute. Add hoisin sauce, oyster sauce, soy sauce and sesame oil. Cook, stirring, for 2 minutes. Add the cornstarch and water mixture, bring to a boil and stir until sauce thickens, about 2 minutes. Remove from heat and stir in pork and scallions. Transfer to a bowl and allow to cool completely.

Punch down dough. Turn out onto a floured work surface and knead until smooth, about 5 minutes. Divide dough into 16 pieces and roll or press out each piece to form a 2¼-inch (6-cm) circle. Cover dough with a damp kitchen towel. Working with one round of dough at a time, spoon 2 teaspoons of filling into the center. Gather edges together, twist to seal and cover with a kitchen towel. Repeat with remaining dough.

Cut out 16 squares of parchment (baking paper) and place buns, sealed side down, on paper. Half fill a medium wok with water (steamer should not touch water) and bring to a boil. Working in batches, arrange buns in steamer, cover and place steamer over boiling water. Steam for 15 minutes, adding more boiling water to wok when necessary. Lift steamer off wok and carefully remove buns. Using scissors, snip the top of each bun twice, to resemble a star. Serve warm with soy sauce and hoisin sauce.

Makes 16

STEAMED PORK BUNS

Lotus nut buns

DOUGH

1½ teaspoons active dry yeast

½ cup (4 fl oz/125 ml) warm water

¼ cup (1¾ oz/50 g) superfine (caster) sugar

1 cup (4 oz/125 g) all-purpose (plain) flour

½ cup (2 oz/60 g) self-rising flour

3 teaspoons butter, melted

FILLING

¾ cup (7½ oz/235 g) canned lotus nut paste

To make dough, in a small bowl, combine yeast with 2 tablespoons warm water, 1 teaspoon sugar and 1 teaspoon all-purpose flour. Mix until well combined. Cover with a kitchen towel and let stand in a warm place until frothy, about 15 minutes.

Sift remaining all-purpose flour and self-rising flour into a large bowl. Add remaining sugar, yeast mixture, remaining warm water and melted butter. Using a wooden spoon, mix to form a soft dough. Turn dough out onto a floured work surface and knead until smooth and elastic, 3–5 minutes. Place dough in a large oiled bowl, cover and let stand in a warm place until doubled in bulk, about 1 hour.

Punch down dough. Turn out onto a floured work surface and knead until smooth, about 5 minutes. Divide dough into 16 pieces and roll or press out each piece to form a 2¼-inch (6-cm) circle. Cover dough with a damp kitchen towel. Working with one round of dough at a time, spoon 2 teaspoons of lotus nut paste into the center. Gather edges together, twist to seal and cover with a kitchen towel. Repeat with remaining dough.

Cut out 16 squares of parchment (baking paper) and place buns, sealed side down, on paper. Half fill a medium wok with water (steamer should not touch water) and bring to a boil. Working in batches, arrange buns in steamer, cover and place steamer over boiling water. Steam for 15–20 minutes, adding more boiling water to wok when necessary. Lift steamer off wok and carefully remove buns. Serve warm.

Makes 16

LOTUS NUT BUNS

Steamed chicken buns

DOUGH

2 1/2 cups (10 oz/300 g) all-purpose (plain) flour

3 teaspoons baking powder

1/2 cup (3 3/4 oz/110 g) superfine (caster) sugar

1/2 cup (4 fl oz/125 ml) milk

1/3 cup (3 fl oz/90 ml) water

1/4 cup (2 fl oz/60 ml) vegetable oil

FILLING

6 Chinese dried mushrooms

1 tablespoon vegetable oil

3 teaspoons peeled and grated fresh ginger

8 oz (250 g) ground (minced) chicken

2 tablespoons chopped, drained canned bamboo shoots

4 scallions (shallots/spring onions), chopped

1 tablespoon oyster sauce

1 teaspoon soy sauce

1 teaspoon Asian sesame oil

1/4 teaspoon salt

2 teaspoons cornstarch (cornflour) mixed with
  2 tablespoons chicken stock

To make dough, sift flour and baking powder into a bowl and add sugar. Gradually add combined milk, water and oil, mixing to form a soft dough. Turn out onto a floured work surface and knead until smooth, 1–2 minutes. Wrap dough in plastic wrap and chill for 1 hour.

To make filling, place mushrooms in a small bowl, add boiling water to cover and allow to stand until softened, 10–15 minutes. Drain, squeeze excess liquid from mushrooms and finely chop, discarding thick stems. Heat oil in a wok or frying pan over medium heat and fry ginger until aromatic, about 1 minute. Add ground chicken and cook until meat changes color, about 3 minutes. Stir in bamboo shoots, scallions, oyster sauce, soy sauce, sesame oil, salt and cornstarch mixture. Bring to a boil and stir until sauce thickens. Remove from heat, transfer filling to a plate and allow to cool completely.

Roll dough into a sausage shape 16 inches (40.5 cm) long. Cut into 16 1-inch (2.5-cm) pieces and roll each into a ball. Cover with a damp kitchen towel. Working with one piece of dough at a time, press into a cup shape. Place 1 tablespoon of filling in the center of dough. Gather edges together, twist and seal. Cover with a damp kitchen towel and repeat with remaining dough.

Cut out 16 squares of parchment (baking paper) and place buns, sealed side down, on paper. Half fill a medium wok with water (steamer should not touch water) and bring to a boil. Working in batches, arrange buns in steamer, cover and place steamer over boiling water. Steam for 20 minutes, adding more boiling water to wok when necessary. Lift steamer off wok and carefully remove buns. Serve with Sweet Cilantro Sauce (page 102).

Makes 16

STEAMED CHICKEN BUNS

Red bean paste buns

DOUGH

1¼ cups (10 oz/300 g) all-purpose (plain) flour

1½ teaspoons baking powder

¼ cup (1¾ oz/50 g) superfine (caster) sugar

¼ cup (2 fl oz/60 ml) milk

2 tablespoons water

1½ tablespoons vegetable oil

FILLING

¾ cup (7½ oz/235 g) canned red bean paste

2 teaspoons black sesame seeds

To make dough, sift flour and baking powder into a bowl and add sugar. Gradually add combined milk, water and oil, mixing to form a soft dough. Turn out onto a floured work surface and knead until smooth, 1–2 minutes. Wrap dough in plastic wrap and chill for 1 hour.

Roll dough into a sausage shape 8 inches (20 cm) long. Cut into 8 1-inch (2.5-cm) pieces and roll each into a ball. Cover with a damp kitchen towel. Working with one piece of dough at a time, press into a cup shape. Place 1 tablespoon of red bean paste in the center of dough. Gather edges together, twist and seal. Cover with a damp kitchen towel and repeat with remaining dough.

Cut out 8 squares of parchment (baking paper) and place buns, sealed side down, on paper. Brush tops of buns with water and sprinkle with black sesame seeds. Half fill a medium wok with water (steamer should not touch water) and bring to a boil. Working in batches, arrange buns in steamer, cover and place steamer over boiling water. Steam for 20 minutes, adding more boiling water to wok when necessary. Lift steamer off wok and carefully remove buns. Serve warm.

Makes 8

RED BEAN PASTE BUNS

Vegetable buns

DOUGH

1½ teaspoons active dry yeast

½ cup (4 fl oz/125 ml) warm water

¼ cup (1¾ oz/50 g) superfine (caster) sugar

1 cup (4 oz/125 g) all-purpose (plain) flour

½ cup (2 oz/60 g) self rising flour

3 teaspoons butter, melted

FILLING

2 tablespoons vegetable oil

1 teaspoon peeled and grated fresh ginger

2 cloves garlic, chopped

4 bunches bok choy, finely chopped

3 bunches choy sum, finely chopped

1 carrot, finely chopped

6 scallions (shallots/spring onions),
  finely chopped

1 teaspoon Asian sesame oil

2 tablespoons Thai sweet chili sauce

To make dough, in a small bowl, combine yeast with 2 tablespoons warm water, 1 teaspoon sugar and 1 teaspoon all-purpose flour. Mix until well combined. Cover with a kitchen towel and let stand in a warm place until frothy, about 15 minutes.

Sift remaining all-purpose flour and self-rising flour into a large bowl. Add remaining sugar, yeast mixture, remaining warm water and melted butter. Using a wooden spoon, mix to form a soft dough. Turn out onto a floured work surface and knead until smooth and elastic, 3–5 minutes. Place dough in a large oiled bowl, cover and let stand in a warm place until doubled in bulk, about 1 hour.

To make filling, heat oil in a wok or frying pan over medium heat and fry ginger and garlic until aromatic, about 1 minute. Add bok choy, choy sum, carrot and scallions. Stir-fry for 2 minutes. Remove from heat and stir in sesame oil and chili sauce. Transfer to a bowl and allow to cool completely.

Punch down dough. Turn out onto a floured work surface and knead until smooth, about 5 minutes. Divide dough into 16 pieces and roll or press out each piece to form a 2¼-inch (6-cm) circle. Cover dough with a damp kitchen towel. Working with one round of dough at a time, spoon 2 teaspoons of filling into the center. Gather edges together, twist to seal and cover with a kitchen towel. Repeat with remaining dough.

Cut out 16 squares of parchment (baking paper) and place buns, sealed side down, on paper. Half fill a medium wok with water (steamer should not touch water) and bring to a boil. Working in batches, arrange buns in steamer, cover and place steamer over boiling water. Steam for 15 minutes, adding more boiling water to wok when necessary. Lift steamer off wok and carefully remove buns. Serve warm with soy sauce, Sweet Cilantro Sauce (page 102), or Chili Sauce (page 100).

Makes 16

VEGETABLE BUNS

wraps

Peking duck pancakes

PANCAKES

³/₄ cup (3 oz/90 g) all-purpose (plain) flour

¹/₃ cup (1¹/₂ oz/45 g) cornstarch (cornflour)

2 eggs, beaten

³/₄ cup (6 fl oz/180 ml) water

¹/₄ cup (2 fl oz/60 ml) milk

2 teaspoons superfine (caster) sugar

1 tablespoon vegetable oil

FILLING

15 scallions (shallots/spring onions)

2 carrots, peeled and cut into thin sticks

1 Chinese roast duck

¹/₄ cup (2 fl oz/60 ml) hoisin sauce

1 tablespoon rice wine

12 chives

¹/₃ cup (3 fl oz/90 ml) hoisin sauce
  for dipping

To make pancakes, sift flour and cornstarch into a bowl. In a separate bowl, whisk together eggs, water, milk and sugar. Make a well in center of dry ingredients, gradually add egg mixture and beat until smooth.

Heat oil in a frying pan over medium heat, pour in 2 tablespoons of pancake batter and swirl pan gently to form a round pancake. Cook until golden, about 2 minutes. Turn and cook other side for 10 seconds. Remove from pan and repeat with remaining batter and oil.

To make filling, cut into each end of scallions with a sharp knife or scissors to form a fringe. Place scallions and carrots in a bowl of iced water and refrigerate for 15 minutes, or until scallions curl. Remove meat and skin from duck and roughly chop. Combine hoisin sauce and rice wine.

Lay pancakes on work surface and place 1 tablespoon of duck meat and skin in center of each one. Top with 1 teaspoon of hoisin and rice wine mixture. Add a scallion curl and 3–4 carrots sticks. Roll and secure with a chive, trimming off any excess chive. Serve with hoisin sauce as a dipping sauce.

Makes 15

PEKING DUCK PANCAKES

Crispy wrapped shrimp

20 jumbo shrimp (green king prawns),
  peeled and deveined, tails intact

2 cloves garlic, finely chopped

2 tablespoons vegetable oil

20 wonton wrappers

1 egg, beaten

20 chives

3 cups (24 fl oz/750 ml) vegetable oil for
  deep-frying

Place shrimp in a bowl, pour in combined garlic and oil, and toss until well coated. Cover and refrigerate for 2 hours. Place wrappers on work surface and cover with a damp kitchen towel. Working with one wrapper at a time, brush edges of wrapper with beaten egg. Place a shrimp diagonally across the center and fold wrapper around shrimp. Place chives in a bowl of hot water for 1 minute, drain and secure wrapper around shrimp with a chive, trimming off excess chive. Cover with a damp kitchen towel and set aside. Repeat with remaining wrappers.

Heat oil in a large wok until it reaches 375°F (190°C) on a deep-frying thermometer, or until a small bread cube dropped in oil sizzles and turns golden. Working in batches, add wrapped shrimp and fry until golden, 1–2 minutes. Using a slotted spoon, remove from oil and drain on paper towels. Serve hot with soy, hoisin or plum sauce.

Makes 20

CRISPY WRAPPED SHRIMP

Lotus leaf wraps

5 dried lotus leaves, cut in half (or use banana leaves or aluminium foil)

1¹/₃ cups (9 oz/280 g) short-grain rice, washed and drained

4 Chinese dried mushrooms

1 tablespoon vegetable oil

2 teaspoons peeled and grated fresh ginger

6¹/₂ oz (200 g) ground (minced) chicken

4 oz (125 g) jumbo shrimp (green king prawns), peeled, deveined and finely chopped

2 Chinese pork sausages, finely chopped

1 tablespoon soy sauce

1 tablespoon rice wine

1 tablespoon oyster sauce

2 teaspoons cornstarch (cornflour) mixed with 1 tablespoon water

The lotus leaves are not eaten; they can be washed carefully and re-used.

Soak lotus leaves in hot water until softened, about 15 minutes. Drain. Line a bamboo steamer with parchment (baking paper), spread drained rice over it and cover steamer. Half fill a medium wok with water (steamer should not touch water) and bring to a boil. Place steamer over boiling water and steam until rice is tender, 25–30 minutes, adding more boiling water to wok when necessary. Remove steamer from wok, allow rice to cool, then divide it into 10 equal portions.

Place mushrooms in a small bowl, add boiling water to cover and let stand until softened, 10–15 minutes. Drain, squeeze excess liquid from mushrooms and finely chop, discarding thick stems.

Heat oil in a wok over medium heat. Fry ginger until aromatic, about 30 seconds. Add chicken and shrimp, and stir-fry until mixture changes color, about 3 minutes. Add sausages, mushrooms, soy sauce, rice wine and oyster sauce, and cook for 1 minute. Stir in cornstarch mixture, bring to a boil and stir until sauce thickens, about 2 minutes. Remove from heat and allow to cool.

Place lotus leaves on work surface. Spoon a portion of rice into the center of each leaf. Place 3 teaspoons of chicken mixture over rice, molding rice around it. Fold leaf over rice to form a parcel and secure with raffia or twine.

Half fill a large wok with water (steamer should not touch water) and bring to a boil. Working in batches, arrange leaf parcels in steamer, cover and place steamer over boiling water. Steam for 15 minutes, adding more boiling water to wok when necessary. Lift steamer off wok and carefully remove parcels. Cut open to serve.

Makes 10

LOTUS LEAF WRAPS

Shrimp pancake rolls

PANCAKES

1¹/₂ cups (6 oz/180 g) all-purpose (plain) flour

2¹/₂ cups (20 fl oz/625 ml) water

2 eggs, beaten

3 tablespoons vegetable oil

FILLING

1 tablespoon oil

2 teaspoons peeled and grated fresh ginger

1 carrot, peeled and grated

1 stick celery, finely chopped

8 oz (250 g) jumbo shrimp (green king prawns),
    peeled, deveined and finely chopped

1 cup (4 oz/125 g) bean sprouts

¹/₄ cup (1¹/₂ oz/45 g) finely chopped cucumber

1 tablespoon soy sauce

1 tablespoon rice wine

1 teaspoon Asian sesame oil

2 teaspoons cornstarch (cornflour)

2 eggs, beaten

3 tablespoons water

2 teaspoons cornstarch (cornflour)

2 tablespoons vegetable oil

To make pancakes, sift flour into a medium bowl. Make a well in center and whisk in combined water and eggs, mixing to form a smooth batter. Heat 2 teaspoons of oil in a non-stick frying pan over medium heat. Add 2 tablespoons of pancake batter and swirl pan gently until pancake sets. Cook until batter bubbles, about 1 minute. Turn and cook other side for 30 seconds. Remove from pan and repeat with remaining batter and oil.

To make filling, heat oil in a wok or frying pan over medium heat and fry ginger until aromatic, about 1 minute. Add carrot, celery and shrimp, and stir-fry until shrimp changes color, about 2 minutes. Remove from heat and add bean sprouts and cucumber. Combine soy sauce, rice wine, sesame oil and cornstarch, add to pan and stir until mixture boils and thickens, 2–3 minutes. Remove from heat, transfer filling to a plate and allow to cool completely.

Lay pancakes on work surface and place 1 tablespoon of filling in center of each one. Fold pancakes over filling to make a neat parcel.

Combine eggs, water and cornstarch in a shallow dish. Heat oil in a frying pan over medium heat. Dip filled pancakes into egg mixture, allowing excess to drain off. Working in batches, fry pancakes until golden on both sides, 2–3 minutes. Repeat with remaining pancakes. Serve hot with soy, hoisin or plum sauce.

Makes 18

SHRIMP PANCAKE ROLLS

Paper-wrapped shrimp rolls

1½ lb (750 g) jumbo shrimp (green king prawns),
    peeled, deveined and finely chopped

3 teaspoons peeled and grated fresh ginger

2 cloves garlic, finely chopped

4 scallions (shallots/spring onions),
    finely chopped

1 tablespoon cornstarch (cornflour)

20 rice paper wrappers, about 8 inches (20 cm)
    square (if unavailable use spring roll wrappers
    or pancakes; see Shrimp Pancake Rolls, page 70)

2 tablespoons cornstarch (cornflour) mixed with
    1½ tablespoons water

¼ cup (2 fl oz/60 ml) vegetable oil for
    deep-frying

In a bowl, combine shrimp, ginger, garlic, scallions and cornstarch. Using wet hands, mix until well combined. Working with one wrapper at a time, plunge it into a shallow bowl of warm water until softened, 1–2 minutes. Lay it on work surface and place 1½ tablespoons of shrimp filling in center. Brush edges of wrapper with combined cornstarch mixture. Fold wrapper over filling, tucking in edges, and roll up to form a neat parcel. Cover with a damp kitchen towel and set aside. Repeat with remaining ingredients.

Heat oil in a wok or frying pan, until it reaches 375°F (190°C) on a deep-frying thermometer, or until a small bread cube dropped in oil sizzles and turns golden. Working in batches, add parcels and fry until golden on both sides, about 2 minutes. Shake pan from time to time to prevent parcels from sticking. Remove from oil and drain on paper towels. Serve hot with hoisin sauce.

Makes 20

PAPER-WRAPPED SHRIMP ROLLS

Stir-fried squid with chili

4 cleaned squid tubes, about 12 oz (375 g) total

2 tablespoons vegetable oil

1 teaspoon Asian sesame oil

3 cloves garlic, finely chopped

1–2 small red chili peppers, seeded and
finely chopped

Cut squid in half lengthwise, then cut into strips ¾ inch (2 cm) wide. Heat oils in a wok or frying pan over medium heat. Fry garlic and chili until aromatic, about 1 minute. Add squid and stir-fry for 1 minute. Do not overcook or squid will become tough. Remove from heat and serve hot.

Makes 4 small servings

Steamed scallops in shells

24 scallops in their shells

2 tablespoons vegetable oil

4 cloves garlic, finely chopped

6 scallions (shallots/spring onions), chopped

GINGER AND SCALLION SAUCE

6 scallions (shallots/spring onions), cut
   into shreds

3 tablespoons vegetable oil

2-inch (5-cm) piece fresh ginger, cut into
   fine shreds

1 green chili pepper, seeded and sliced

4 tablespoons soy sauce

2 tablespoons water

Clean scallops and return to shells. Heat oil in a small saucepan over medium heat and fry garlic until aromatic, about 1 minute. Add scallions and cook for 1 minute. Remove from heat. Spoon garlic and scallions over scallops.

Half fill a medium wok with water (steamer should not touch water) and bring to a boil. Working in batches, arrange scallops in a bamboo steamer, cover and place steamer over boiling water. Steam until scallops are tender, 7–10 minutes, adding more boiling water to wok when necessary. Lift steamer off wok and carefully remove scallops.

To make ginger and scallion sauce, place scallions in a small bowl and set aside. Heat oil in a small saucepan over medium heat and fry ginger and chili until aromatic, about 1 minute. Remove from heat and stir in soy sauce and water. Bring to a boil and pour over scallions. Let stand for 2 minutes before serving with scallops.

Makes 4 small servings

STEAMED SCALLOPS IN SHELLS

Shrimp balls

1 lb (500 g) jumbo shrimp (green king prawns), peeled and deveined

2 cloves garlic

3 teaspoons peeled and grated fresh ginger

2 teaspoons fish sauce

¹/₄ teaspoon salt

¹/₄ cup (1 oz/30 g) cornstarch (cornflour), plus extra for coating

4 scallions (shallots/spring onions), roughly chopped

2 tablespoons finely chopped canned water chestnuts

¹/₄ cup (2 oz/60 g) finely chopped canned bamboo shoots

3 cups (24 fl oz/750 ml) vegetable oil for deep-frying

lime wedges for serving

These shrimp balls can be steamed or deep-fried.

Place shrimp, garlic, ginger, fish sauce, salt and cornstarch in a food processor and process until smooth. Transfer to a bowl. Stir in scallions, water chestnuts and bamboo shoots. Using wet hands, mix until well combined.

Coat hands in cornstarch and form 1 tablespoon of shrimp mixture into a ball. Toss shrimp ball in cornstarch, shaking off any excess. Repeat with remaining mixture.

Heat oil in a large wok until it reaches 375°F (190°C) on a deep-frying thermometer, or until a small bread cube dropped in oil sizzles and turns golden. Working in batches, add shrimp balls and fry until golden, about 2 minutes. Using a slotted spoon, remove from oil and drain on paper towels. Serve hot with lime wedges and Lime and Fish Sauce (page 105).

The shrimp balls may be threaded onto skewers after cooking.

Makes 12

SHRIMP BALLS

Clams with black bean sauce

1 lb (500 g) fresh clams in shells, shells cleaned

BLACK BEAN SAUCE

2 teaspoons vegetable oil

2 cloves garlic, finely chopped

2 teaspoons peeled and grated fresh ginger

2 teaspoons fermented black beans, rinsed
  and chopped

2 tablespoons soy sauce

1/3 cup (3 fl oz/90 ml) water

2 tablespoons oyster sauce

Place clams in a bamboo steamer and cover with lid. Half fill a medium wok with water (steamer should not touch water) and bring to a boil. Place steamer over boiling water and steam until clam shells open, 3–4 minutes (discard any clams that do not open). Lift steamer off wok and carefully remove clams.

To make black bean sauce, heat oil in a small saucepan over medium heat. Fry garlic and ginger until aromatic, about 1 minute. Add black beans, soy sauce, water and oyster sauce. Bring to a boil, reduce heat and simmer for 1 minute. Serve drizzled over clams.

Serves 6–8

CLAMS WITH BLACK BEAN SAUCE

Steamed pork ribs

1 lb (500 g) pork spareribs, trimmed and cut into
   3¹/₄-inch (8-cm) lengths (ask your butcher to
   prepare these for you)

1 tablespoon rice wine

1 teaspoon salt

2 teaspoons superfine (caster) sugar

1 teaspoon Asian sesame oil

4 cloves garlic, finely chopped

2 tablespoons fermented black beans, washed
   and chopped

¹/₂ teaspoon dry chili flakes

2 teaspoons cornstarch (cornflour)

¹/₂ red bell pepper (capsicum), seeded and
   finely shredded

Place ribs in a shallow dish. Combine rice wine, salt, sugar, sesame oil, garlic, black beans, chili flakes and cornstarch and mix well. Pour over ribs, cover and refrigerate for 2 hours.

Half fill a medium wok with water (steamer should not touch water) and bring to a boil. Working in batches, place ribs on a heatproof plate and put it into a bamboo steamer. Cover and place steamer over boiling water. Steam until ribs are tender, about 25 minutes, adding more boiling water to wok when necessary. Lift steamer off wok and carefully remove ribs. Garnish with shredded red bell pepper.

Makes 8 small servings

STEAMED PORK RIBS

Barbecue pork, Chinese style

2 pork fillets, 12 oz (375 g) each

3 tablespoons hoisin sauce

3 tablespoons ground bean sauce

2 cloves garlic, crushed

1/4 teaspoon Chinese five-spice powder

3 tablespoons soy sauce

pinch of Chinese red food coloring powder
  (optional)

1 tablespoon brown sugar

This recipe can be used in dishes where Chinese barbecue pork is required; see Steamed Pork Buns, page 54.

Place pork fillets in a shallow dish. Combine hoisin sauce, ground bean sauce, garlic, five-spice powder, soy sauce, red food coloring and brown sugar, and mix well. Pour over pork and toss until well coated in marinade. Cover and refrigerate overnight.

Drain pork and reserve marinade. Place pork on a wire rack over a baking dish. Bake at 350°F (180°C/Gas 4) for 30 minutes, basting with marinade and turning pork during cooking. Remove from oven and allow to stand for 10 minutes before slicing. Serve hot or cold.

Makes 8 small servings

BARBECUE PORK, CHINESE STYLE

Chinese vegetables with oyster sauce

2 tablespoons oyster sauce

3 tablespoons chicken stock

2 teaspoons soy sauce

1 teaspoon Asian sesame oil

1 teaspoon cornstarch (cornflour) mixed with
   1 tablespoon chicken stock

1 bunch garlic chives, tied into a bundle with
   string, or choy sum or bok choy, trimmed into
   4-inch (10-cm) lengths and tied with string

In a small saucepan, combine oyster sauce, stock, soy sauce, sesame oil and cornstarch mixture. Bring to a boil over medium heat, stirring until sauce bubbles and thickens. Remove from heat.

Blanch garlic chives or Chinese vegetables in a saucepan of boiling water for 1 minute. Remove from pan with a slotted spoon, place on serving plate and remove string. Tie one of the chives around bundle, pour oyster sauce over it and serve.

Serves 4

CHINESE VEGETABLES WITH OYSTER SAUCE

Grilled mushrooms

13 oz (400 g) shiitake mushrooms, stems trimmed

2 tablespoons soy sauce

2 tablespoons mirin

1 tablespoon superfine (caster) sugar

1 tablespoon chopped chives

2 teaspoons black sesame seeds mixed with

  1 teaspoon chopped chives

Place mushrooms in a shallow dish. Combine soy sauce, mirin, sugar and chives, and pour over mushrooms. Cover and marinate for 5 minutes. Drain mushrooms and reserve marinade.

Place mushrooms on a lightly oiled tray and cook under a preheated hot broiler (grill) until softened, about 3 minutes on each side. Brush with marinade during cooking. Arrange mushrooms in small bowls or plates, and sprinkle with black sesame seed and chive mixture. Serve hot.

Makes 4 small servings

Mini vegetable spring rolls

1 tablespoon vegetable oil

2 cloves garlic, finely chopped

2 teaspoons peeled and grated fresh ginger

6 scallions (shallots/spring onions),
  finely chopped

2 stalks celery, finely chopped

2 cups (8 oz/250 g) grated carrot

2 cups (6 oz/180 g) shredded Chinese
  green cabbage

1 cup (4 oz/125 g) bean sprouts

3 tablespoons finely chopped, drained canned
  water chestnuts

1/2 cup (3/4 oz/20 g) finely chopped fried
  bean curd

3 teaspoons cornstarch (cornflour) mixed with
  1 tablespoon water

2 teaspoons Asian sesame oil

2 teaspoons soy sauce

20 frozen mini spring roll wrappers, about
  4 1/2 inches (11.5 cm) square, thawed

extra 2 teaspoons cornstarch (cornflour) mixed
  with 2 tablespoons water

4 cups (32 fl oz/1 L) vegetable oil for deep-frying

Heat oil in a wok over medium heat. Add garlic and ginger, and cook until aromatic, about 1 minute. Stir in scallions, celery, carrot and cabbage. Cook until vegetables soften, about 3 minutes. Add bean sprouts, water chestnuts and fried bean curd. Cover and cook for 2 minutes. Pour in cornstarch mixture, sesame oil and soy sauce, bring to a boil, reduce heat and cook, stirring, until sauce thickens, 1–2 minutes. Remove from heat, transfer to a plate and allow to cool completely.

Separate spring roll wrappers, place on a work surface and cover with a damp kitchen towel. Working with one wrapper at a time and using your fingertips, wet edges with extra cornstarch and water mixture. Place 1 tablespoon of filling in center of wrapper and roll up diagonally, tucking in edges. Seal edges with cornstarch and water mixture. Repeat with remaining wrappers.

Heat oil in a large wok until it reaches 375°F (190°C) on a deep-frying thermometer, or until a small bread cube dropped in oil sizzles and turns golden. Working in batches, add rolls and fry until golden, about 1 minute. Using a slotted spoon, remove from oil and drain on paper towels. Serve hot with Easy Plum Sauce (page 104).

Makes 20

MINI VEGETABLE SPRING ROLLS

desserts

Chinese custard tarts

PASTRY

3 cups (12 oz/375 g) all-purpose (plain) flour

6 oz (180 g) lard

5 tablespoons hot water

FILLING

3 eggs, beaten

1/3 cup (2 oz/ 60 g) superfine (caster) sugar

1 1/2 cups (12 fl oz/375 ml) milk

yellow food coloring (optional)

To make pastry, sift flour into a bowl. Using your fingertips, rub lard into flour, until mixture resembles coarse breadcrumbs. Add hot water and mix to form a firm dough. Turn dough out onto a floured work surface and knead until smooth. Roll out between 2 sheets of parchment (baking paper) to 1/8 inch (3 mm) thick. Using a 3-inch (8-cm) round cutter, cut dough into 24 rounds. Line greased tart (patty) pans with dough.

To make filling, beat eggs, sugar, milk and a few drops of food coloring (if using) together until smooth. Pour into prepared pastry. Bake at 425°F (220°C/Gas 7) for 10 minutes. Reduce oven temperature to 400°F (200°C/Gas 6) and bake until custard is set, 10–15 minutes. Remove from oven and allow to stand for 10 minutes before transferring to a wire rack to cool. Serve cold or chilled.

Makes 24

CHINESE CUSTARD TARTS

Fresh mango pudding

4 ripe mangoes, peeled and pitted

1/4 cup (2 fl oz/ 60 ml) orange juice

1 cup (8 fl oz/250 ml) water

1/3 cup (2 oz/60 g) superfine (caster) sugar

6 teaspoons gelatin

mango slices for serving

Place mango and orange juice in a food processor and process until smooth. Strain through a coarse sieve and set aside.

Place water, sugar and gelatin in a saucepan. Stir over low heat until sugar and gelatin dissolve. Remove from heat and allow to cool for 5 minutes. Stir in mango pulp and mix well. Pour into serving glasses or 6 individual jelly molds and refrigerate until firm, 2–3 hours. If in molds, turn out onto serving plates. Garnish with mango slices.

Serves 6

FRESH MANGO PUDDING

Sweet coconut bars

2½ cups (17½ oz/545 g) glutinous rice

2¼ cups (18 fl oz/560 ml) coconut milk

½ cup (3¼ oz/110 g) superfine (caster) sugar

TOPPING

1¼ cups (5 oz/150 g) unsweetened shredded
   (desiccated) coconut

¼ cup (2 fl oz/60 ml) coconut milk, warmed

3 oz (90 g) grated palm sugar or brown sugar

3 tablespoons water

Place rice in a large bowl, cover with cold water and let stand overnight.

Line a large bamboo steamer with parchment (baking paper) and spread drained rice on top. Cover steamer.

Half fill a medium wok with water (steamer should not touch water) and bring to a boil. Place steamer over boiling water and steam until rice is tender, about 45 minutes, adding more boiling water to wok when necessary.

Place steamed rice into a medium, heavy-bottomed saucepan. Add coconut milk and sugar. Stir over low heat until the coconut milk has been absorbed, about 10 minutes. Evenly spread rice into a shallow baking pan about 7½ by 11 inches (19 by 28 cm) lined with parchment (baking paper). Refrigerate until firm, about 2 hours.

To make topping, combine coconut and coconut milk. Place palm sugar and water in a small saucepan and stir over low heat until mixture thickens slightly, 3–4 minutes. Pour into coconut and milk mixture and stir until well combined. Allow to cool to room temperature.

Spread topping over rice and refrigerate for 1 hour. Cut into small squares to serve.

Makes 16 pieces

SWEET COCONUT BARS

Almond pudding

2 cups (16 fl oz/500 ml) cold water

1/3 cup (2 oz/60 g) superfine (caster) sugar

5 teaspoons gelatin

2/3 cup (5 fl oz/160 ml) evaporated milk

1/2 teaspoon almond extract

mango slices for serving

These tiny gelatic squares can be served with any fresh fruit.

Place water and sugar in a saucepan. Sprinkle gelatin over top. Bring mixture to a boil, stirring for 1 minute. Remove from heat. Add evaporated milk and almond extract, and mix well. Pour into an oiled pan about 7½ by 11 inches (18 by 28 cm). Refrigerate until firm, 2–3 hours. Cut into small squares and serve with slices of fresh mango.

Makes 16

ALMOND PUDDING

sauces

Sweet cilantro sauce

1/4 cup (2 oz/60 g) superfine (caster) sugar

3/4 cup (6 fl oz/180 ml) white vinegar

1/4 cup (2 fl oz/60 ml) water

1 small red chili pepper, seeded and sliced

2 scallions (shallots/spring onions), sliced

1 tablespoon finely chopped cilantro (coriander)

1/2 small cucumber, seeded and chopped

Place sugar, vinegar and water in a small saucepan. Stir over low heat until sugar dissolves. Remove from heat and stir in chili, scallions, cilantro and cucumber.

Makes 1 cup (8 fl oz/250 ml)

Ginger soy dipping sauce

3 teaspoons peeled and grated fresh ginger

1/2 cup (4 fl oz/125 ml) light soy sauce

2 tablespoons Thai sweet chili sauce

Combine ginger, soy sauce and chili sauce and mix well.

Makes ⅔ cup (5 fl oz/150 ml)

Chili sauce

2 teaspoons sambal oelek

1/2 cup (4 fl oz/125 ml) rice wine

1 teaspoon superfine (caster) sugar

1 tablespoon finely chopped scallions (shallots/spring onions)

Combine sambal oelek, rice wine, sugar and scallions, and mix well.

Makes ½ cup (4 fl oz/125 ml)

Lime and cilantro dipping sauce

2 tablespoons fish sauce

2 tablespoons white vinegar

2 tablespoons fresh lime juice

1/2 teaspoon superfine (caster) sugar

2 tablespoons finely chopped cilantro (coriander)

Combine fish sauce, vinegar, lime juice, sugar and cilantro, and mix well.

Makes 1/4 cup (2 fl oz/60 ml)

Easy plum sauce

5 tablespoons plum jam

½ cup (4 fl oz/125 ml) rice wine vinegar

1 small red chili pepper, seeded and thinly sliced

Place jam and vinegar in a small saucepan and stir over medium heat until jam melts, about 3 minutes. Remove from heat and allow to cool. Just before serving, stir chili into sauce.

Makes 1 cup (8 fl oz/250 ml)

Quick sweet-and-sour sauce

1½ cups (12 fl oz/375 ml) pineapple juice

2 tablespoons tomato ketchup

2 teaspoons tomato paste (concentrate)

2 tablespoons superfine (caster) sugar

3 tablespoons white vinegar

Place all ingredients in a medium saucepan and bring to a boil. Reduce heat to low and simmer for 10 minutes, stirring occasionally. Remove from heat and allow to cool before serving.

Makes 1½ cups (12 fl oz/375 ml)

Lime and fish sauce

1/2 cup (4 fl oz/125 ml) lime juice

2 teaspoons grated palm sugar or brown sugar

2 teaspoons fish sauce

1 teaspoon finely chopped scallion
  (shallot/spring onion)

1 teaspoon finely chopped, seeded red
  chili pepper

1 teaspoon peeled and grated fresh ginger

Place lime juice in a bowl. Add sugar and stir until sugar dissolves. Add fish sauce, scallion, chili and ginger, and mix well.

Makes 1/2 cup (4 fl oz/125 ml)

Glossary

bean curd. Also known as tofu, bean curd is made from soaked yellow soybeans ground into a puree and cooked in water. A coagulant is added to the resultant soy milk, the whey is drained off and the curds are lightly pressed. Fresh bean curd is available in soft or firm varieties. Once open, store in a bowl of water in the refrigerator. Bean curd is sold in the refrigerated section of Asian markets.

bean sprouts. Sprouting green mung beans, sold fresh or canned. Fresh sprouts tend to have a crisper texture and a more delicate flavor. Store in refrigerator for up to 3 days.

black beans. These salted and fermented soybeans are available in cans or packets from Asian markets. They should be rinsed before use as they can be very salty. Store unused black beans in a covered container in refrigerator.

Chinese barbecue pork. Also known as cha siu. Boneless pork that has been marinated in Chinese five-spice powder and soy sauce, and then roasted. Sold in slices or strips in Chinese markets. Store up to 2 days in refrigerator.

Chinese roast duck. Sold freshly roasted in Chinese markets and delicious in stir-fries or on its own. Use 1–2 days after purchase. Substitute roast chicken if unavailable.

cilantro. Pungent, fragrant leaves from the coriander plant, resembling parsley and also called Chinese parsley and fresh coriander. Leaves and roots are used widely in Southeast Asian cuisine.

coconut milk. Rich liquid extracted from shredded coconut that has been steeped in water. It is used in sweet and savory Asian dishes. Coconut milk is available canned.

fish sauce. Pungent sauce of salted fermented fish and other seasonings. Products vary in intensity depending on the country of origin. Fish sauce from Thailand, called nam pla, is a commonly available variety.

five-spice powder. This fragrant blend of spices is used extensively in Chinese cooking. It contains star anise, Sichuan peppercorns, fennel, cloves and cinnamon. Use sparingly.

ginger. Thick, rootlike rhizome of the ginger plant, with a sharp, pungent flavor. Once the thin, tan skin is peeled from fresh ginger, the flesh is grated or sliced. Store fresh ginger in refrigerator for up to 3 days.

gow gee press. A special (usually plastic) utensil for making gow gee (semicircular dumplings). Presses are sold in Asian markets.

ground bean sauce. A commercial sauce made from soybeans, sugar, salt, sesame oil and flour and sold in Asian markets.

lotus nut paste. Traditionally used as the filling for Chinese moon cakes, lotus nut paste is made from the seeds of the lotus plant. It is sold in cans in Asian markets.

mirin. Sweet alcoholic wine made from rice. Store in a cool, dark place after opening. Sweet sherry can be substituted.

palm sugar. Dense, heavy, dark cakes made from the sap of palm trees and sold in Asian markets. Shave with a sharp knife or grate before using. Substitute brown sugar if unavailable.

red bean paste. Boiled, mashed and sweetened azuki beans, sold in cans in Asian markets.

oyster sauce. Thick, dark brown Chinese sauce made from fermented dried oysters and soy sauce, and used to impart an intense or mild briny flavor to stir-fries and other dishes. Store in refrigerator after opening.

sambal oelek. Spicy Indonesian paste consisting of ground chili peppers combined with salt and occasionally vinegar. It can be used as a substitute for fresh chili peppers.

soy sauce. Salty sauce made from fermented soybeans and usually wheat, used as an ingredient and as a table condiment. Dark soy sauce is thicker and often less salty than light soy sauce. Low-sodium products are also available.

Thai sweet chili sauce. Mild, sweet chili sauce used as a flavoring and as a dipping sauce. Store in refrigerator after opening.

Index

Guide to weights and measures

The conversions given in the recipes in this book are approximate. Whichever system you choose, the important thing to remember is to ensure the balance remains the same throughout the ingredients. If you follow all the metric measures, you will end up with the same proportions as if you followed all the imperial.

DRY MEASURES

Imperial	Metric
⅙ oz	5 g
½ oz	15 g
1 oz	30 g
2 oz	60 g
3 oz	90 g
3½ oz	100 g
4 oz (¼ lb)	125 g
5 oz	150 g
6 oz	180 g
6½ oz	200 g
7 oz	220 g
8 oz (½ lb)	250 g
9 oz	280 g
10 oz	300 g
11 oz	330 g
12 oz (¾ lb)	375 g
13 oz	400 g
14 oz	440 g
15 oz	470 g
16 oz (1 lb)	500 g
24 oz (1½ lb)	750 g
32 oz (2 lb)	1 kg
3 lb	1.5 kg
4 lb	2 kg

LIQUID MEASURES

Imperial	Metric	Cup
1 fl oz	30 ml	
2 fl oz	60 ml	¼ cup
3 fl oz	90 ml	⅓ cup
4 fl oz	125 ml	½ cup
5 fl oz	150 ml	⅔ cup
6 fl oz	180 ml	¾ cup
8 fl oz	250 ml	1 cup
10 fl oz	300 ml	1½ cups
14 fl oz	450 ml	2 cups
16 fl oz	500 ml	2 cups
24 fl oz	750 ml	
32 fl oz	1000 ml (1 litre)	4 cups

USEFUL CONVERSIONS

¼ teaspoon	1.25 ml
½ teaspoon	2.5 ml
1 teaspoon	5 ml
1 Australian tablespoon	20 ml (4 teaspoons)
1 UK/US tablespoon	15 ml (3 teaspoons)

Butter/Shortening

1 tablespoon	½ oz	15 g
1½ tablespoons	¾ oz	20 g
2 tablespoons	1 oz	30 g
3 tablespoons	1½ oz	50 g

OVEN TEMPERATURE GUIDE

The Celsius and Fahrenheit temperatures in this chart relate to most electric ovens. Decrease by 25°F or 10°C for gas ovens or refer to the manufacturer's temperature guide. For temperatures below 325°F (160°C), do not decrease the given temperature.

Oven Description	Celsius °C	Fahrenheit °F	Gas Mark
Cool	100	200	¼
Very slow	120	250	½
Slow	150	300	2
Warm	160	325	3
Moderate	180	350	4
Moderately hot	190	375	5
Moderately hot	200	400	6
Hot	220	425	7
Very hot	230	450	8
Extremely hot	250	500	10

First published in the United States in 1999 by Periplus Editions (HK) Ltd., with editorial offices at
153 Milk Street, Boston, Massachusetts 02109 and 5 Little Road #08-01, Singapore 536983.

Library of Congress Catalog Card Number: 99-60843

ISBN: 962 593 528 2

DISTRIBUTED BY

USA
Tuttle Publishing
Distribution Center
Airport Industrial Park
364 Innovation Drive
North Clarendon, VT 05759-9436
Tel: (802) 773-8930
Tel: (800) 526-2778

CANADA
Raincoast Books
9050 Shaughnessy Street
Vancouver
British Columbia
V6P 6E5
Tel: (604) 323-7100
Fax: (604) 323-2600

JAPAN
Tuttle Publishing
RK Building, 2nd Floor
2-13-10 Shimo-Meguro, Meguro-Ku
Tokyo 153 0064
Tel: (03) 5437-0171
Fax: (03) 5437 0755

SOUTHEAST ASIA
Berkeley Books Pte. Ltd.
5 Little Road #08-01
Singapore 536983
Tel: (65) 280-3320
Fax: (65) 280-6290

First edition
05 04 03 02 01 00   10 9 8 7 6 5 4 3

Printed in Singapore